ARE WE THERE YET?

36 Eye-Rolling Flowcharts from the Wonderfully Weird Brains of Children

By David Vienna

KNOCK
KNOCK.®
VENICE, CALIFORNIA

Created, published, and distributed by Knock Knock
1635 Electric Ave.
Venice, CA 90291
knockknockstuff.com
Knock Knock is a registered trademark of
Knock Knock LLC

Illustrations by Denis Carrier

This book is meant solely for entertainment purposes. In no event will Knock Knock be liable to any reader for any harm, injury, or damages, including direct, indirect, incidental, special, consequential, or punitive, arising out of or in connection with the use of the information contained in this book.

So there.

ISBN: 978-168349080-7
UPC: 825703-50241-1

10 9 8 7 6 5 4 3 2 1

Hello.

For parents, nothing makes sense. I mean it. Nothing.

When trying to get your offspring out the door, they slow to a pace seen only in land-based mollusks. When serving dinner, your child inexplicably considers their favorite dish super gross. And just helping your son or daughter get dressed may include a debate over whether or not a chipmunk costume is appropriate attire for a visit from Aunt Bea. Logic, it seems, escapes your kid's decision-making process.

But that's not true.

Kids have a refined intellectual method...well, not refined, really, and not at all intellectual, but certainly a method for figuring out things like which color marker to use on the wall or how much sugar is too much. Collected within these pages, you'll find riveting examples of common situations faced by children and exactly how they apply their... let's call it unique inner dialogue to land on the path that's right for them in that moment.

Of course, all of that is subject to change at any time. They're kids, after all, not robots. Obviously, robots do what they're told.

So the next time the kids do something that makes you think they've gone crazy, feral, or are just possessed, flip through the pages of this book for some guidance. It doesn't mean your kid isn't actually possessed, but at least you'll have some reassurance that a demon did not make young Kevin throw the container of building blocks down the stairs. No, that was a decision he came to on his own.

—David Vienna

Do I Need More Sugar?

What have you eaten so far?

An entire bag of gummy bears

Three cupcakes

A hot fudge sundae

A whole chocolate Easter Bunny and/or Santa

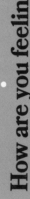

Pop Rocks and cherry cola

How are you feeling?

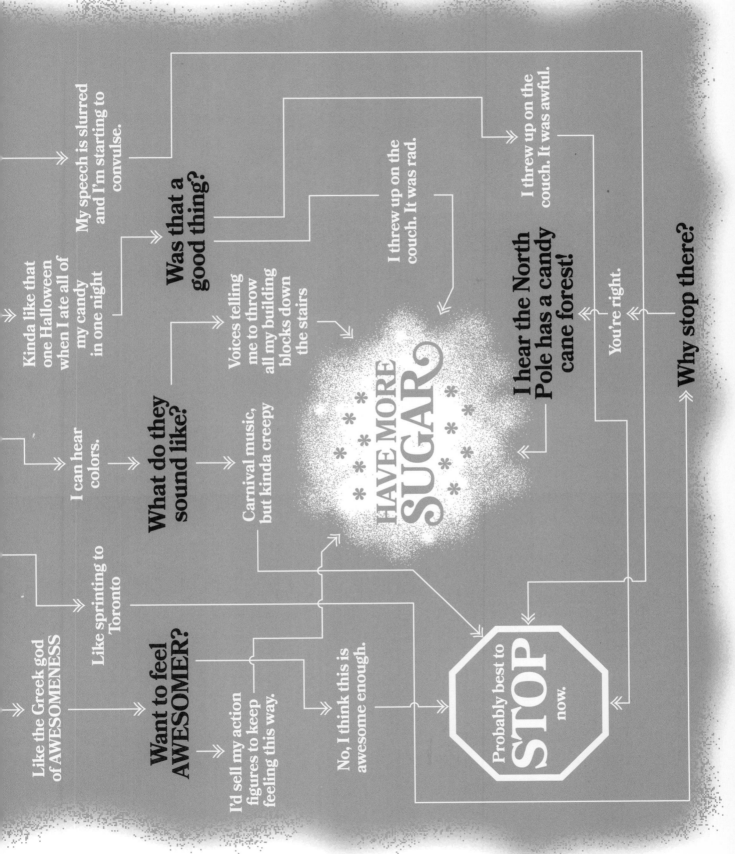

HAVE MORE SUGAR

Like the Greek god of AWESOMENESS

Want to feel AWESOMER?

I'd sell my action figures to keep feeling this way.

No, I think this is awesome enough.

Like sprinting to Toronto

I can hear colors.

What do they sound like?

Carnival music, but kinda creepy

Voices telling me to throw all my building blocks down the stairs

Kinda like that one Halloween when I ate all of my candy in one night

My speech is slurred and I'm starting to convulse.

Was that a good thing?

I threw up on the couch. It was rad.

I threw up on the couch. It was awful.

I hear the North Pole has a candy cane forest!

You're right.

Why stop there?

Probably best to **STOP** now.

WHAT'S IN MY CLOSET?

WHAT TIME IS IT?

Day

Night

CLOTHES AND STUFF

CHILD-EATING MONSTER

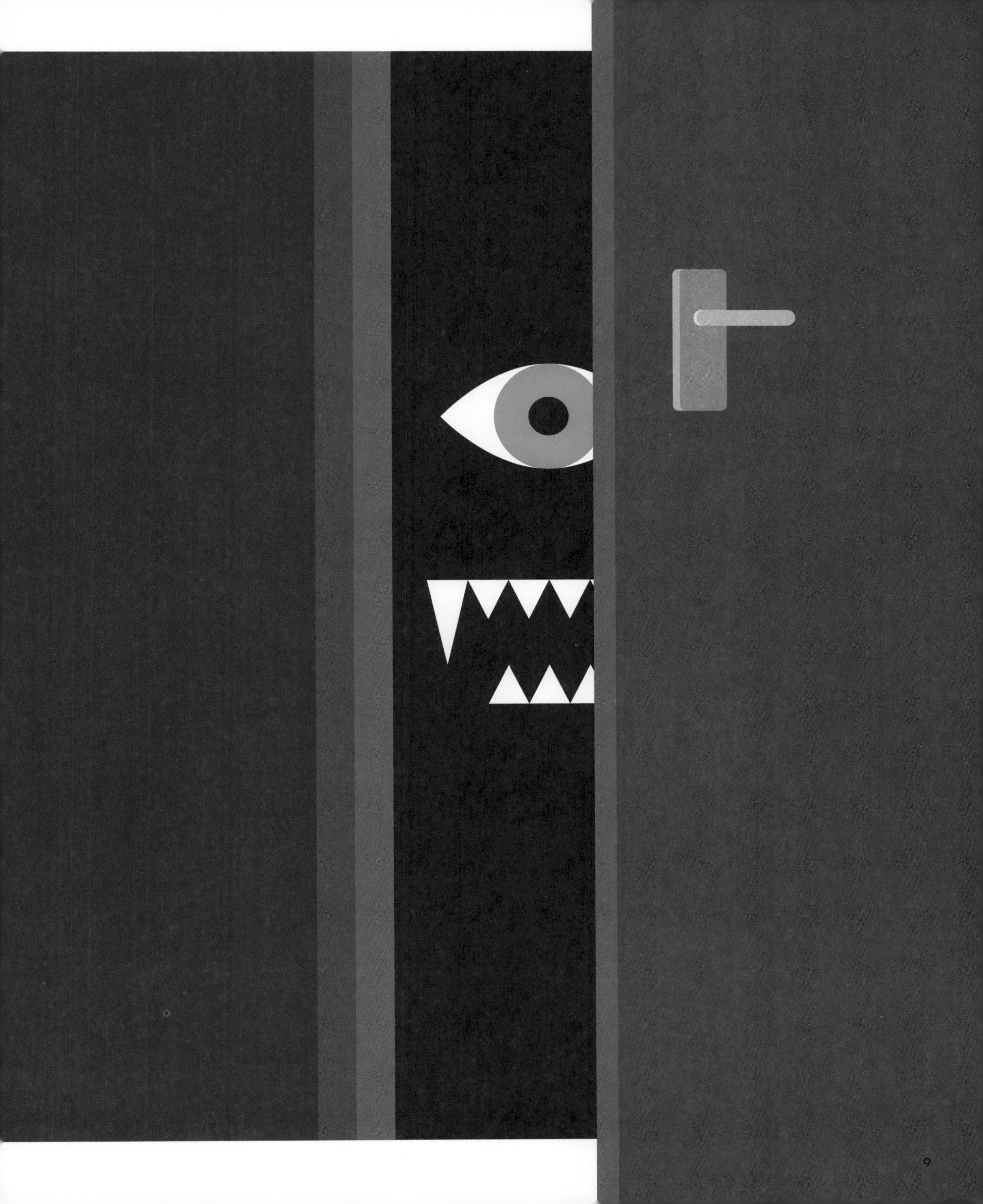

Should I Bother Mom While She's in the Bathroom?

What is she doing?

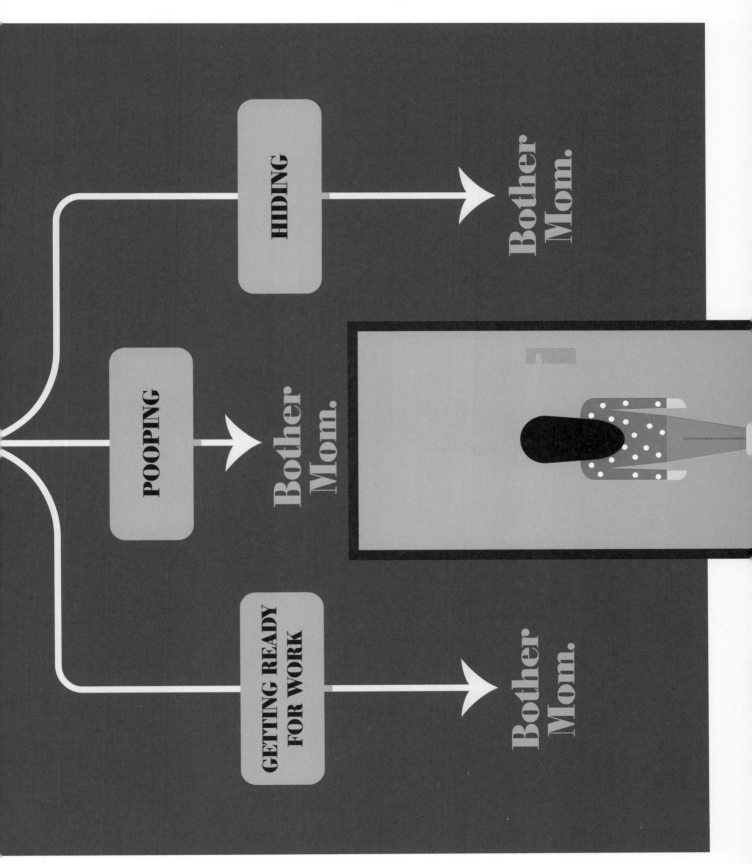

SHOULD I DRESS UP THE DOG?

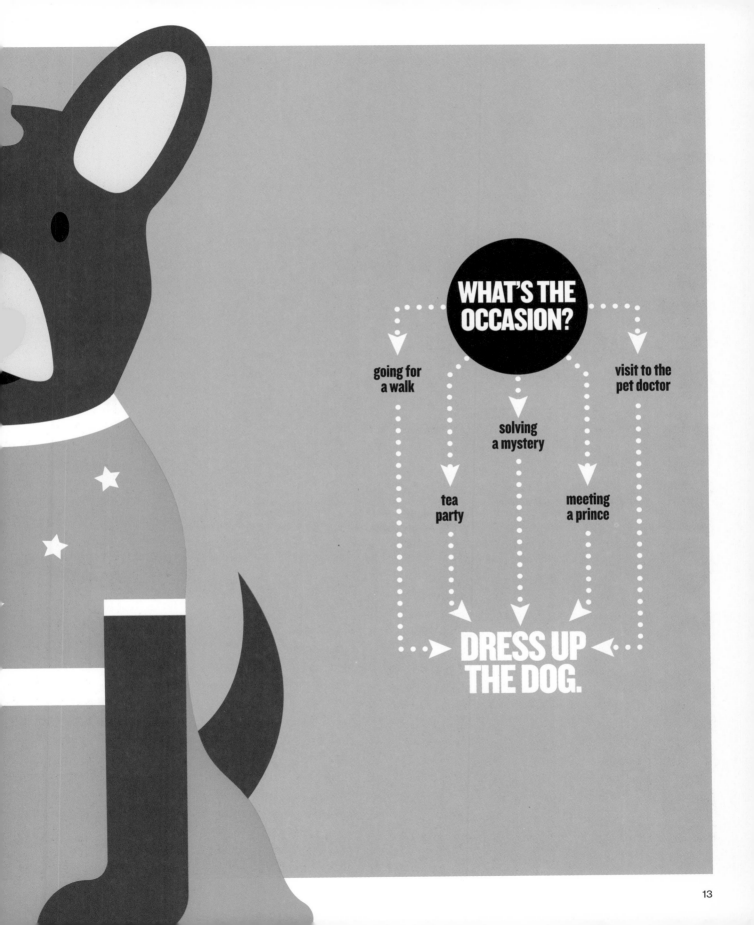

WHAT'S THE OCCASION?

going for a walk

visit to the pet doctor

solving a mystery

tea party

meeting a prince

DRESS UP THE DOG.

HOW LONG SHOULD I BRUSH MY TEETH?

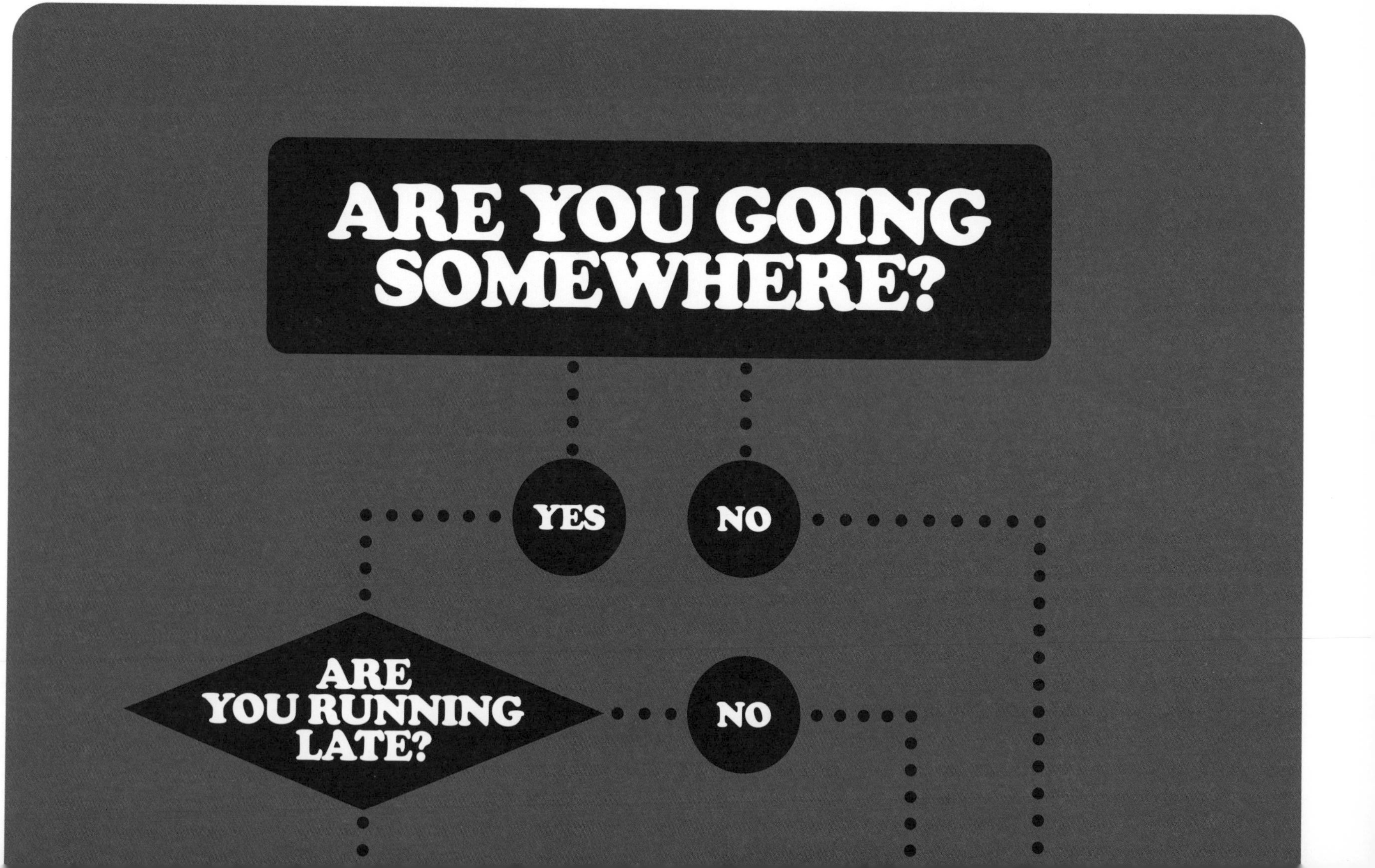

ARE YOU GOING SOMEWHERE?

YES

NO

NO

ARE YOU RUNNING LATE?

BRUSH FOR 10 SECONDS.

YES

BRUSH FOR 10 MINUTES.

SHOULD I THROW THIS?

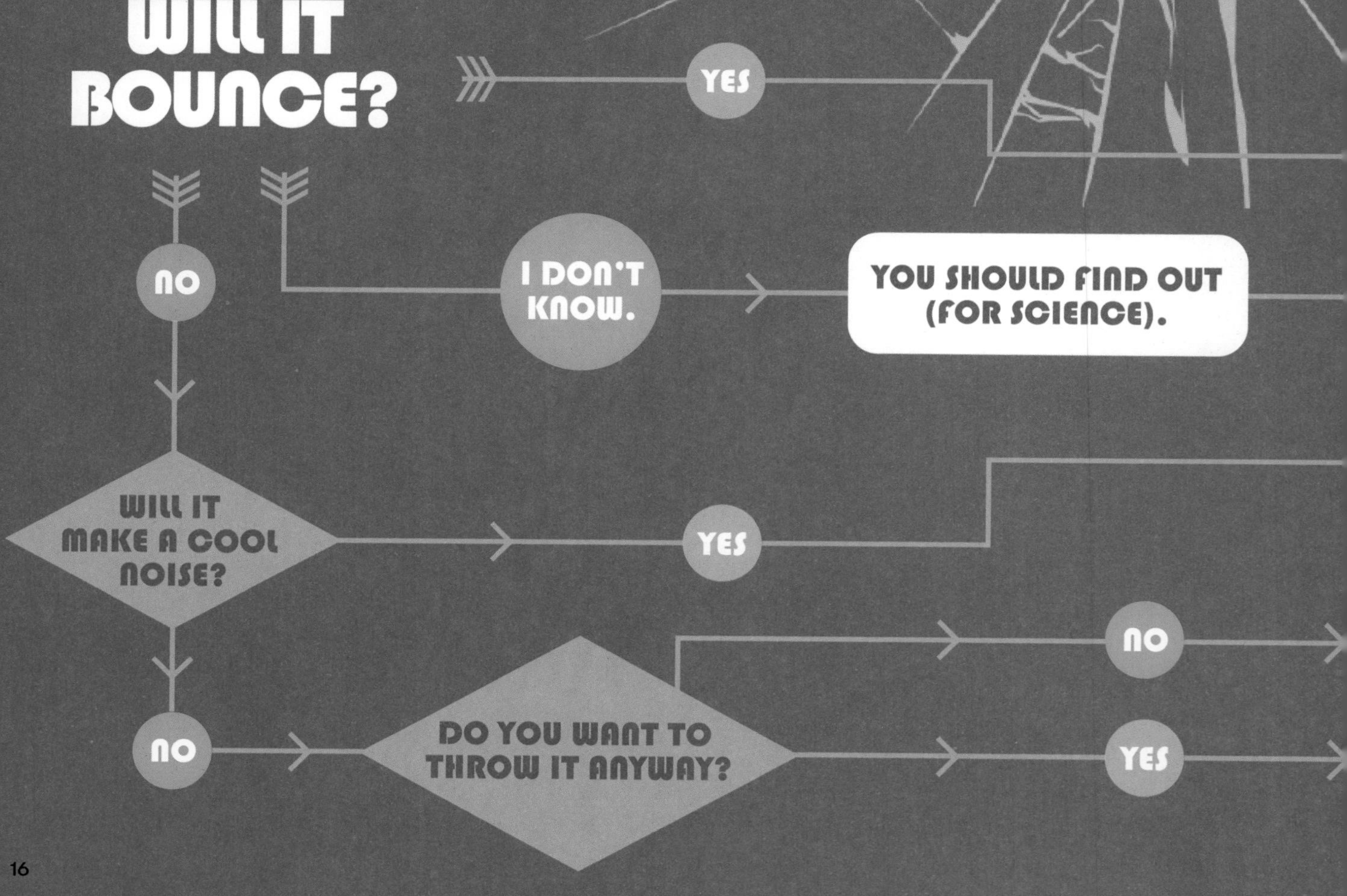

WILL IT BOUNCE?

>>> YES

NO

I DON'T KNOW.

→ YOU SHOULD FIND OUT (FOR SCIENCE).

WILL IT MAKE A COOL NOISE?

YES

NO

NO

DO YOU WANT TO THROW IT ANYWAY?

YES

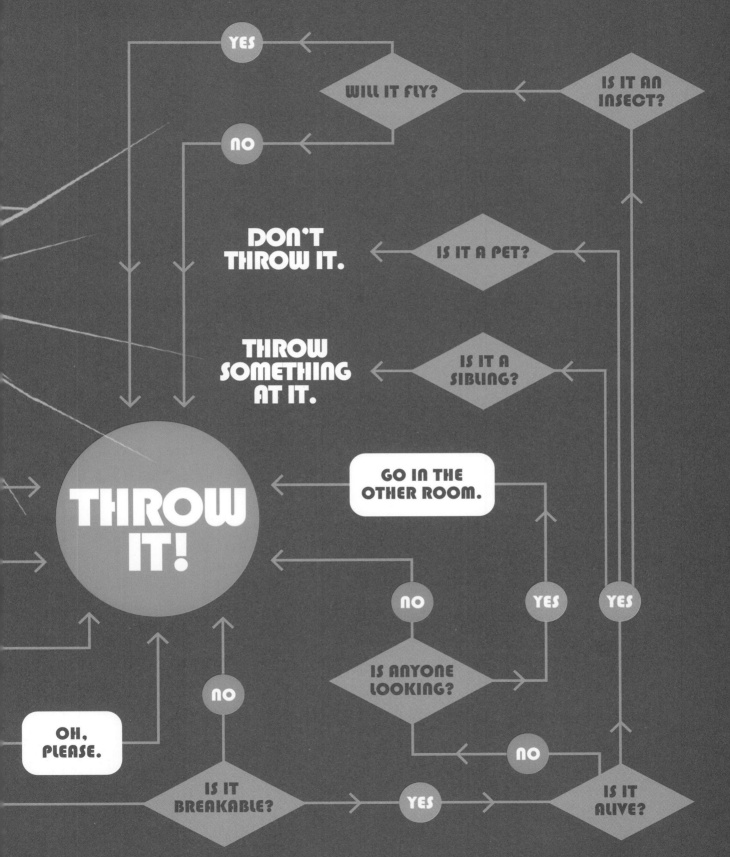

17

DID I FL
THE TOI

WHAT DID YOU PUT IN IT?

- PEE → **IS THE WATER YELLOW?**
  - LIKE LEMONADE
  - HOW YELLOW EXACTLY?
- POO → **IS THE POO STILL THERE?**
  - YUP
  - I CAN'T TELL BECAUSE THE TOILET PAPER I USED IS IN THE WAY.
- MAYBE A TOY CAR... OR FOUR → **THEN WHAT HAPPENED?**
- BARBIE'S HEAD → **CAN YOU STILL SEE IT?**

USH
LET?

YOU DIDN'T
FLUSH.

THE CARS
MIGHT HAVE
DISAPPEARED.

THE TOILET
MIGHT HAVE
OVERFLOWED.

SEE WHAT?

JUST HER HAIR

YOU
FLUSHED.

Should I Use

What are y

Sandwich

Cake

Pasta

Use your hands.

My Utensils?

ou eating?

Filet

Soup

Nothing, I just want to make a boatload of noise.

Use your utensils.

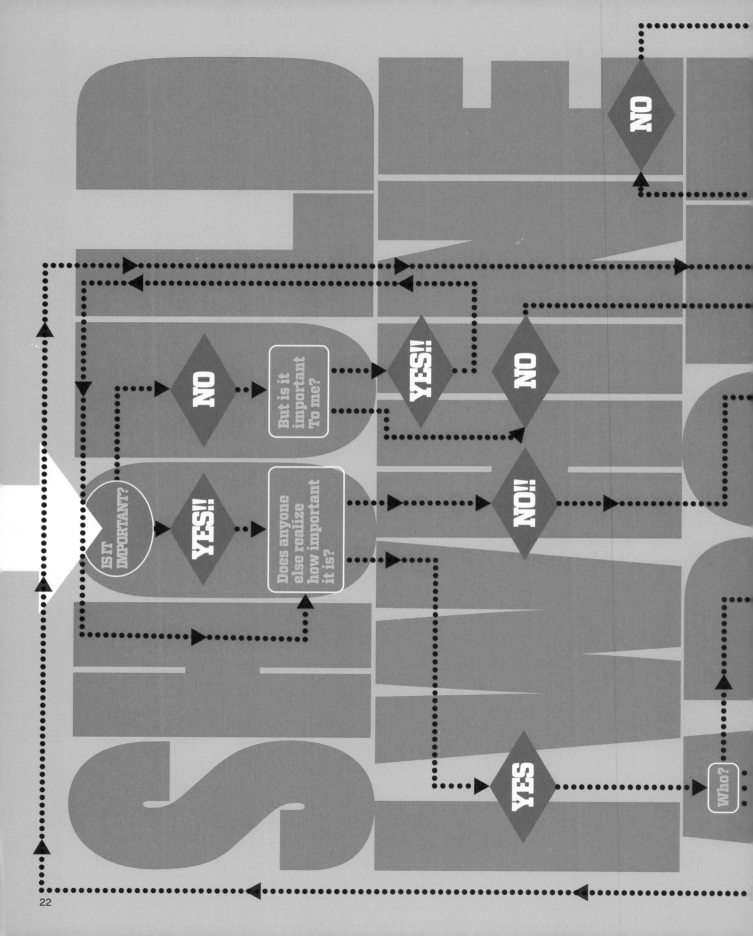

IS IT IMPORTANT?

NO

YES!!

But is it important To me?

Does anyone else realize how important it is?

YES!!

NO

NO!!

NO

YES

Who?

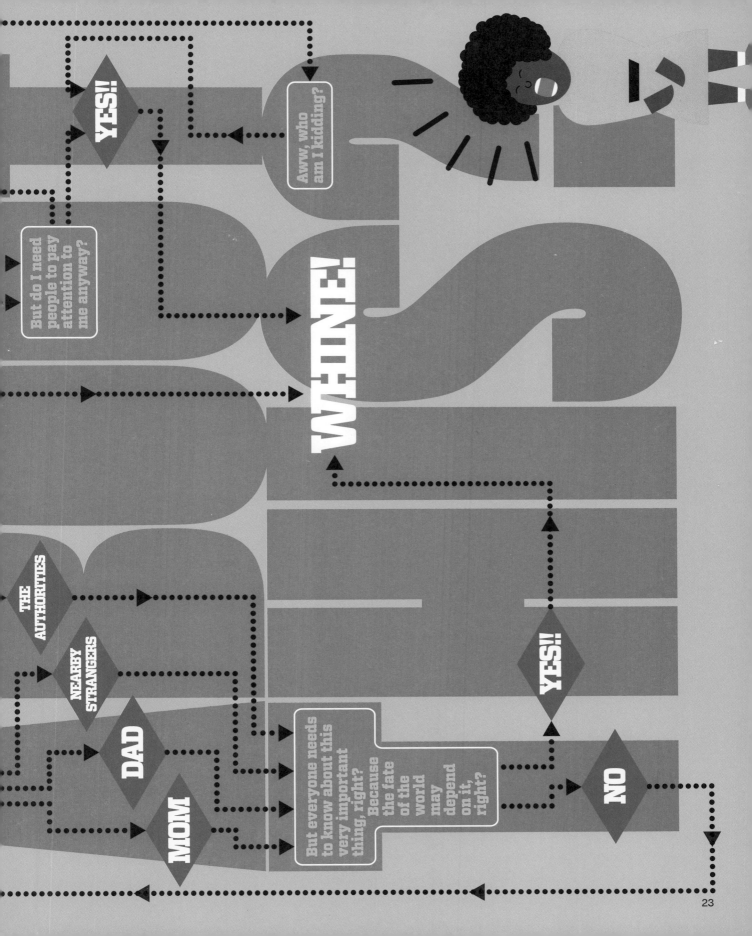

YES!!

But do I need people to pay attention to me anyway?

Aww, who am I kidding?

WHINE!

THE AUTHORITIES

NEARBY STRANGERS

DAD

MOM

But everyone needs to know about this very important thing, right? Because the fate of the world may depend on it, right?

YES!!

NO

JUST KINDA HUNGRY.

IS YOUR LITTLE BROTHER ASKING FOR CRACKERS, TOO?

YES

NO

HOW HUNGRY ARE YOU?

HOW GRAHAM SHOULD

YES ··▸ HOW LONG UNTIL DINNER?

I'M ABOUT TO DIE OF STARVATION.

IS IT ALMOST DINNER TIME?

NO

SHOULD WE ALERT THE AUTHORITIES?

BUT WHO KNOWS WHEN
YOU'LL BE FED AGAIN? ········▶ EXACTLY! ·····

MANY
RACKERS
I EAT?

EAT
ALL OF
THEM.

MINUTES

AN HOUR

PROBABLY

DO THEY DELIVER
GRAHAM CRACKERS? ·····▶ NO ·····

SHOULD I GET OUT OF BED?

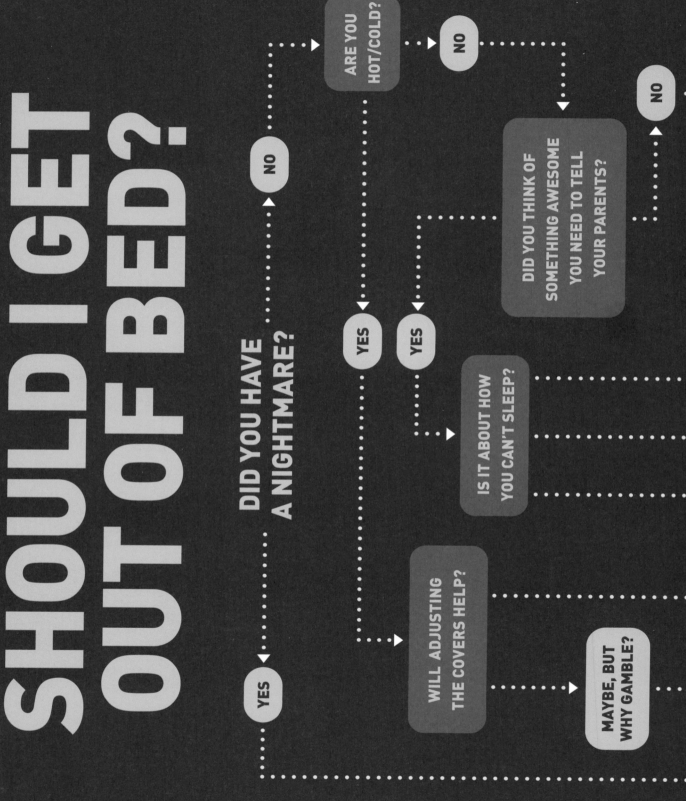

DID YOU HAVE A NIGHTMARE?

NO

YES

ARE YOU HOT/COLD?

NO

YES

YES

DID YOU THINK OF SOMETHING AWESOME YOU NEED TO TELL YOUR PARENTS?

NO

IS IT ABOUT HOW YOU CAN'T SLEEP?

WILL ADJUSTING THE COVERS HELP?

MAYBE, BUT WHY GAMBLE?

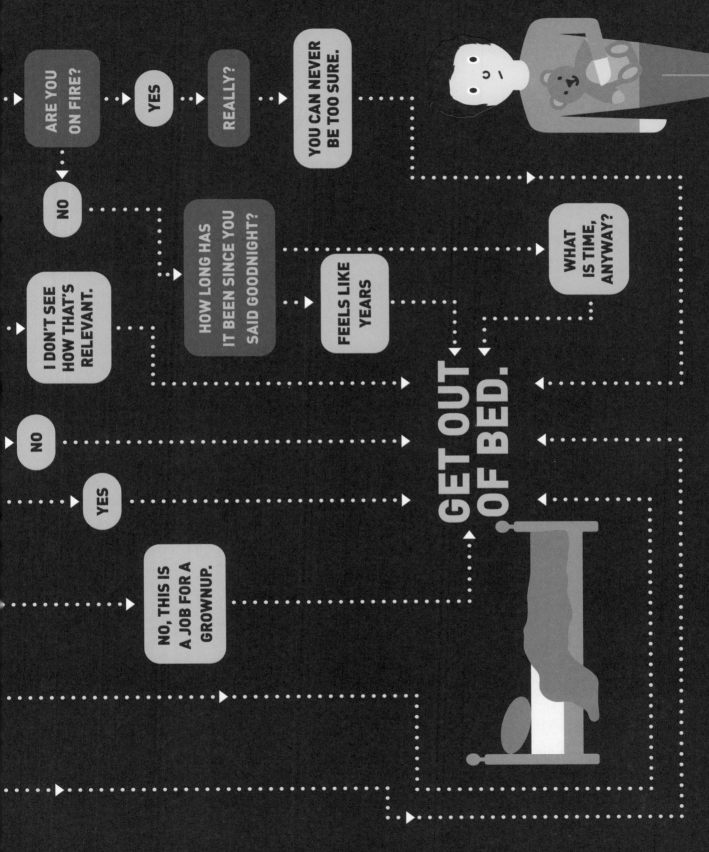

WHERE IS MY OTHER SHOE?

DID YOU LOOK IN YOUR ROOM?

YES

NO → LOOK IN YOUR ROOM.

IT'S NOT THERE.

DID YOU CHECK UNDER THE BED?

NO → CHECK UNDER YOUR BED.

YES

DID YOU SEE ANYTHING SHOE-SHAPED?

YES → YES

IS IT POSSIBLE THAT OBJECT IS SOMETHING OTHER THAN YOUR SHOE?

YES

NO

NO

YOU FOUND YOUR SHOE.

IT'S THE WRONG SHOE.

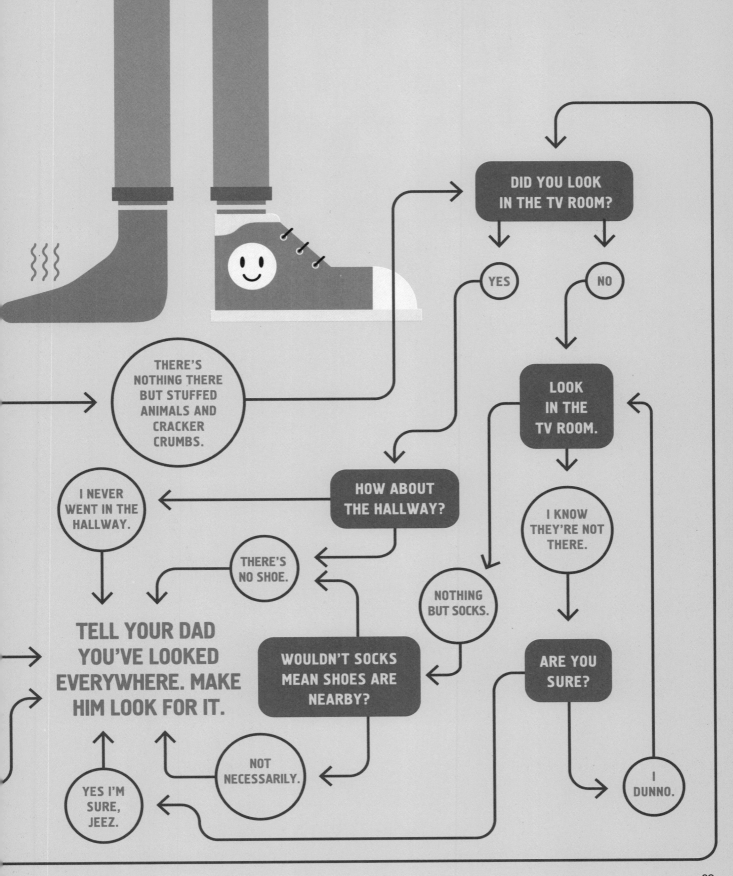

SHOULD I CUT MY OWN HAIR?

DO YOU THINK YOU CAN GIVE YOURSELF A SUPER AWESOME HAIRCUT?

YES.

ARE YOU SURE?

YES.

WHY?

BECAUSE I SAW HOW THE LADY AT THE HAIRCUT PLACE DID IT.

BUT SHE WENT TO SCHOOL FOR THAT.

I'M IN SCHOOL.

THAT'S A DIFFERENT KIND OF SCHOOL.

I'M DOING IT.

MAYBE YOU SHOULD HOLD—

DID IT!

HOW'S IT LOOK?

FANTASTIC. NOW HOW DO I PUT IT BACK?

PICK A SPECIALTY. → STRENGTH

STEALTH

ACROBATICS

Do you have a ninja costume?

Can you do a somersault? — NO

YES — NO

YES

Do a somersault over one of these:

Do you have a shirt you can wear on your head like a mask?

Couch

Laundry pile

Cat

Put it on.

YES — NO

Put on mask.

Go naked!

Sneak up on Mom while her arms are full, jump out, and yell, "Hee-ya!"

YOU'RE

OME A NINJA?

Can you vanquish a foe?

YES → **How big of a foe?**

NO → **Do you have something you can use as a sword?**

How about a jumping kick?

NO → **Just do a jump then.**

YES → **Do repeated jumping kicks at bedtime.**

How big of a foe?

- **Sibling-sized** → **Tackle and pin.**
- **Dad-sized** → **Punch him in the butt.**

Do you have something you can use as a sword?

NO → **Yes, you do—it's called your hand.**

YES → **Use it to chop one of these in half.**

- **Houseplant**
- **Meatball sub**
- **Banana**

A NINJA!

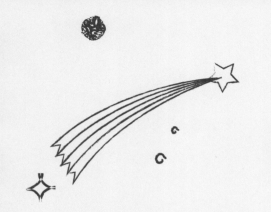

IS IT COOL HOMEWORK?

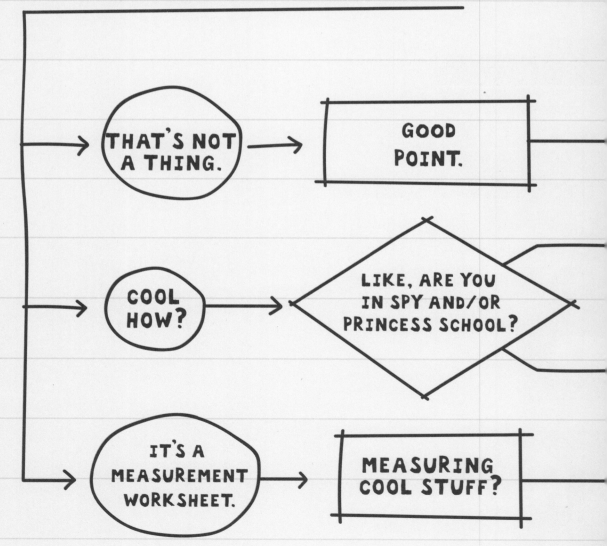

THAT'S NOT A THING.

GOOD POINT.

COOL HOW?

LIKE, ARE YOU IN SPY AND/OR PRINCESS SCHOOL?

IT'S A MEASUREMENT WORKSHEET.

MEASURING COOL STUFF?

D I DO EWORK?

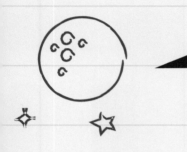

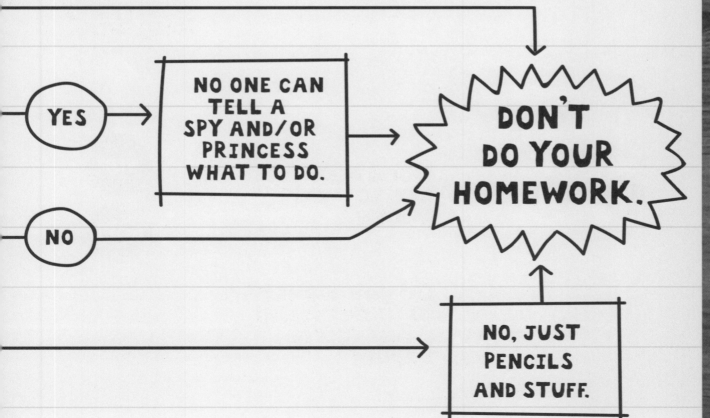

YES → NO ONE CAN TELL A SPY AND/OR PRINCESS WHAT TO DO. → DON'T DO YOUR HOMEWORK.

NO →

NO, JUST PENCILS AND STUFF. ↑

Is he into collecting stuff?

Talk about Harry Potter for a really long time.

Y **N**

Does he like to read books?

YUP

NOPE

Do you want him to understand what you're saying?

SHOULD DAD

2

Talk about Pokémon for a really long time.

Talk about Shopkins for a really long time.

Attempt to tell a joke you heard at school, but can't quite remember.

SURE

NOT REALLY

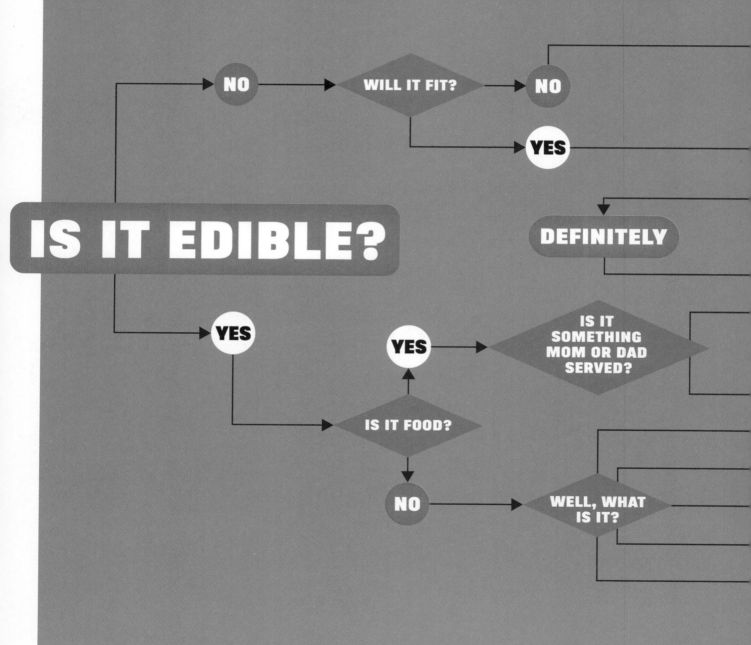

SHOULD I PUT TH

NO → WILL IT FIT? → NO

YES

DEFINITELY

IS IT EDIBLE?

YES

YES → IS IT SOMETHING MOM OR DAD SERVED?

IS IT FOOD?

NO → WELL, WHAT IS IT?

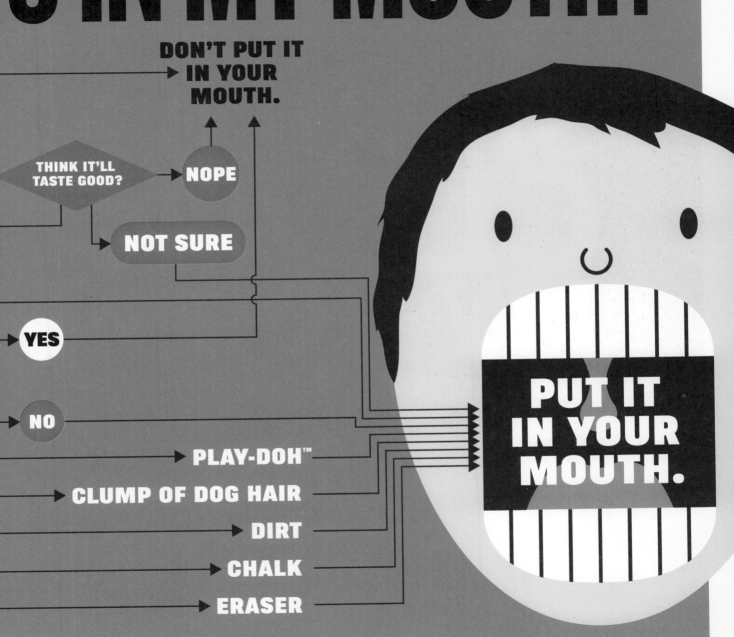

S IN MY MOUTH?

SHOULD I CLEAN MY ROOM

LIKE MOM ASKED ME TO?

WERE YOU ALREADY DOING SOMETHING?

YES

NO

Rolling down the stairs

Pretending to be a tiger

Eat a snack.

Just sit here.

WHAT?

WHAT WOULD YOU RATHER DO?

Making an epic couch fort

Throwing ice cubes into the ceiling fan

Watch a movie.

Play a game.

Playing tennis in the hallway

Dance.

KEEP DOING THAT.

DO THAT.

AND DON'T CLEAN YOUR ROOM.

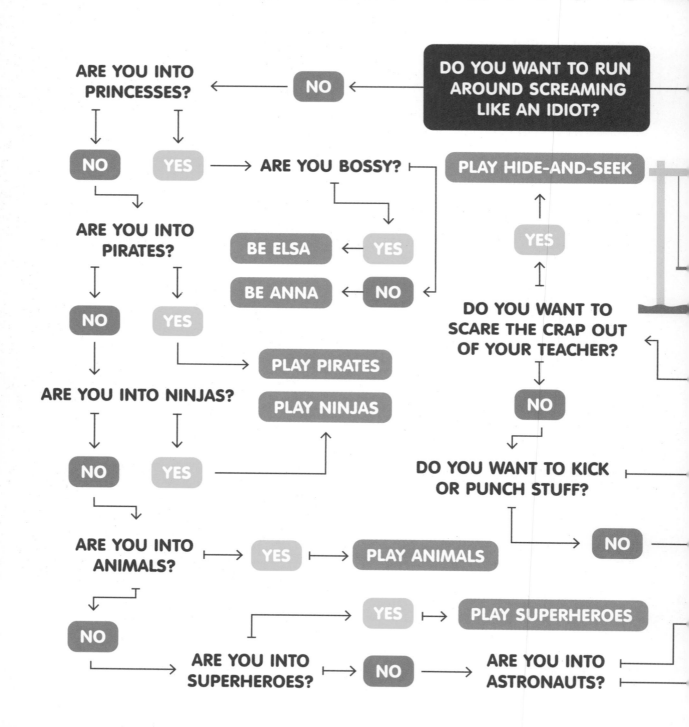

ARE YOU INTO PRINCESSES?

DO YOU WANT TO RUN AROUND SCREAMING LIKE AN IDIOT?

NO

NO   YES → ARE YOU BOSSY?

PLAY HIDE-AND-SEEK

ARE YOU INTO PIRATES?

BE ELSA ← YES

BE ANNA ← NO

YES

DO YOU WANT TO SCARE THE CRAP OUT OF YOUR TEACHER?

NO   YES

PLAY PIRATES

PLAY NINJAS

NO

ARE YOU INTO NINJAS?

NO   YES

DO YOU WANT TO KICK OR PUNCH STUFF?

NO

ARE YOU INTO ANIMALS?   YES → PLAY ANIMALS

NO

YES → PLAY SUPERHEROES

NO

ARE YOU INTO SUPERHEROES?   NO   ARE YOU INTO ASTRONAUTS?

D I PLAY AT RECESS?

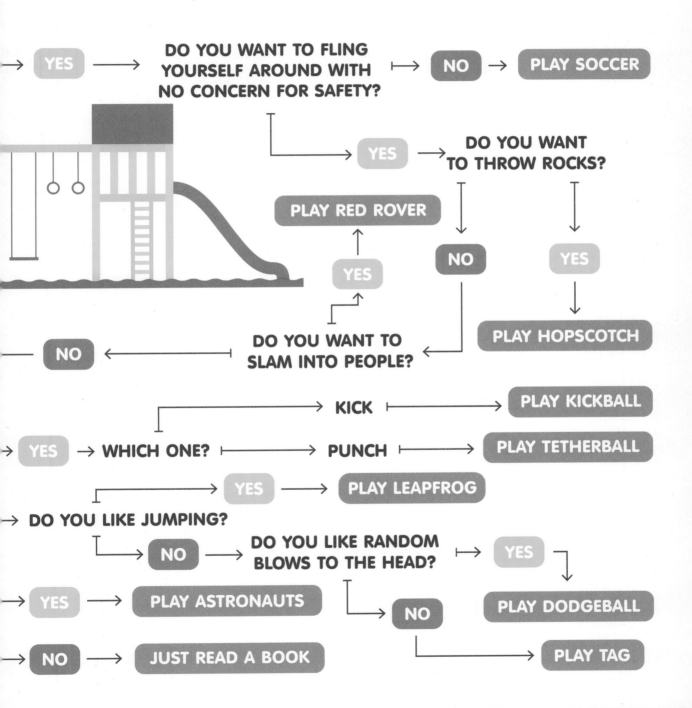

YES → DO YOU WANT TO FLING YOURSELF AROUND WITH NO CONCERN FOR SAFETY? → NO → PLAY SOCCER

YES → DO YOU WANT TO THROW ROCKS?

PLAY RED ROVER

YES

NO   YES

DO YOU WANT TO SLAM INTO PEOPLE?

PLAY HOPSCOTCH

NO

KICK → PLAY KICKBALL

YES → WHICH ONE? → PUNCH → PLAY TETHERBALL

YES → PLAY LEAPFROG

DO YOU LIKE JUMPING?

NO → DO YOU LIKE RANDOM BLOWS TO THE HEAD? → YES

YES → PLAY ASTRONAUTS

NO → PLAY DODGEBALL

NO → JUST READ A BOOK

PLAY TAG

IS GRILLED CHEESE ITS OWN FOOD GROUP?

WOULD YOU EAT ANYTHING OTHER THAN GRILLED CHEESE?

NOPE.

I GUESS I'D ALSO EAT A COUPLE OF SLICES OF MELTED CHEESE BETWEEN PIECES OF TOAST.

THAT'S A GRILLED CHEESE.

YES, IT'S A FOOD GROUP.

WHAT SHOULD I WEAR

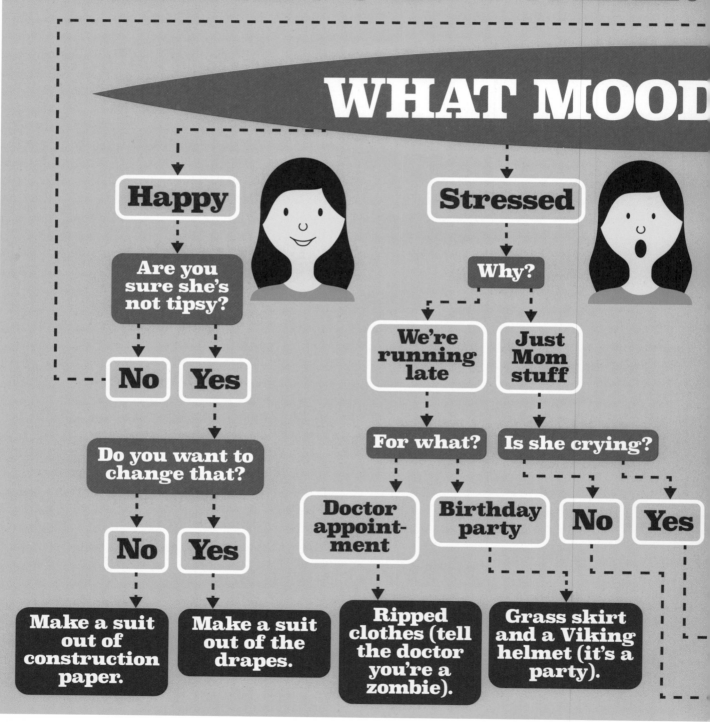

WHAT MOOD

Happy

Are you sure she's not tipsy?

No   Yes

Do you want to change that?

No   Yes

Make a suit out of construction paper.

Make a suit out of the drapes.

Stressed

Why?

We're running late   Just Mom stuff

For what?   Is she crying?

Doctor appointment   Birthday party   No   Yes

Ripped clothes (tell the doctor you're a zombie).

Grass skirt and a Viking helmet (it's a party).

WITH MY NEW SHOES?

IS MOM IN?

Mad

Is she mad at you?

Yes ← **Yes** **No**

Was that the plan?

Lederhosen

No

Raid her closet and make an elf costume, you mischievous sprite.

Cape (she needs a hero).

Raincoat

Wait, you have lederhosen? Wear them ALL THE TIME.

Tipsy

What's the occasion?

It's Saturday

Grandma and Grandpa are coming over

Pajamas

Nothing except the shoes.

Also, now's a good time to ask for ice cream.

WHAT DOES IT TASTE LIKE?

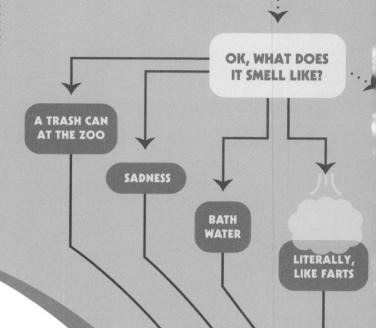

OK, WHAT DOES IT SMELL LIKE?

A TRASH CAN AT THE ZOO

SADNESS

BATH WATER

LITERALLY, LIKE FARTS

LIMA BEANS

ASPARAGUS

WHAT'S THIS THING ON MY PLATE?

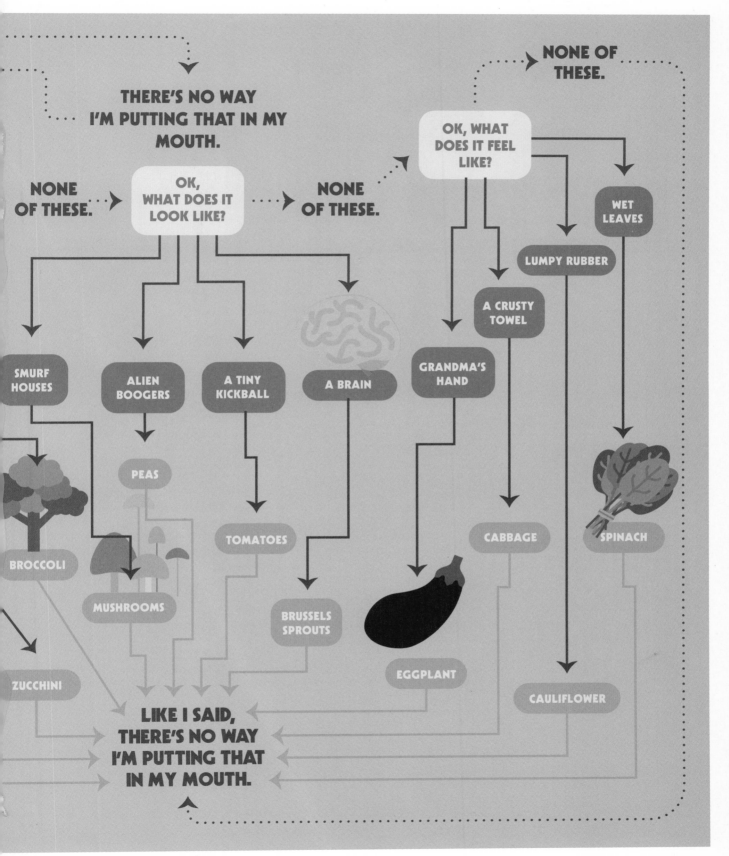

HOW SHOULD I SHOW MY FRUSTRATION?

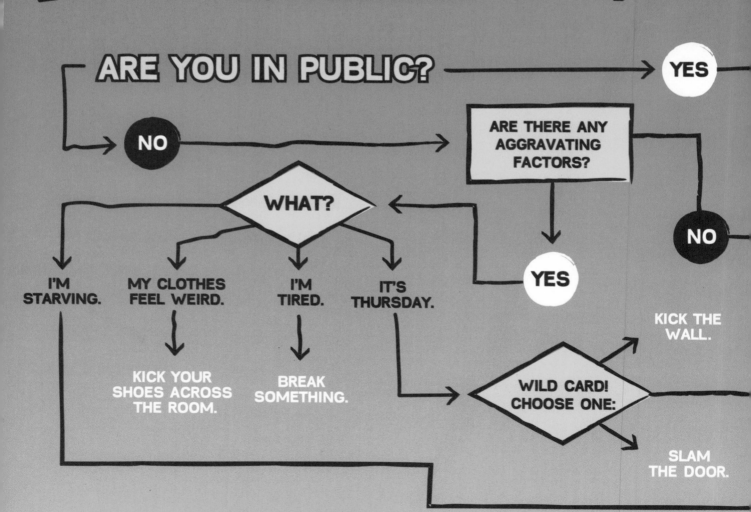

ARE YOU IN PUBLIC? → YES

NO →

ARE THERE ANY AGGRAVATING FACTORS?

WHAT?

YES

NO

I'M STARVING.

MY CLOTHES FEEL WEIRD. → KICK YOUR SHOES ACROSS THE ROOM.

I'M TIRED. → BREAK SOMETHING.

IT'S THURSDAY.

WILD CARD! CHOOSE ONE: → KICK THE WALL. / SLAM THE DOOR.

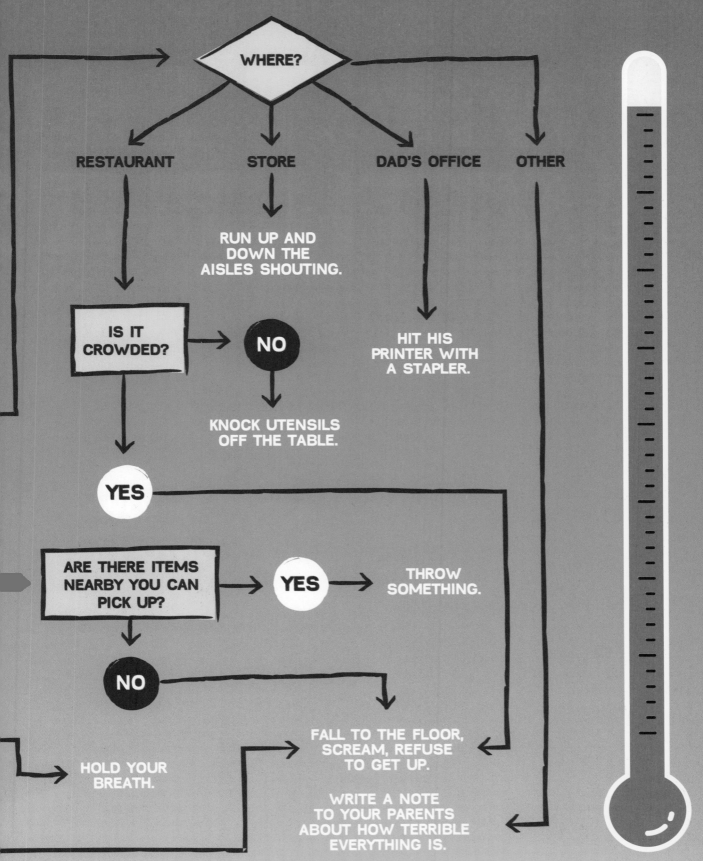

WHAT SHO
WITH THIS

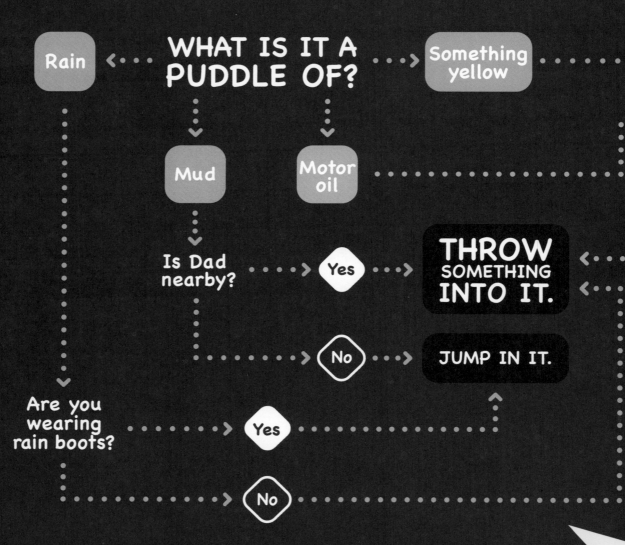

Rain

WHAT IS IT A PUDDLE OF?

Something yellow

Mud

Motor oil

Is Dad nearby?

Yes

No

THROW SOMETHING INTO IT.

JUMP IN IT.

Are you wearing rain boots?

Yes

No

OULD I DO
S PUDDLE?

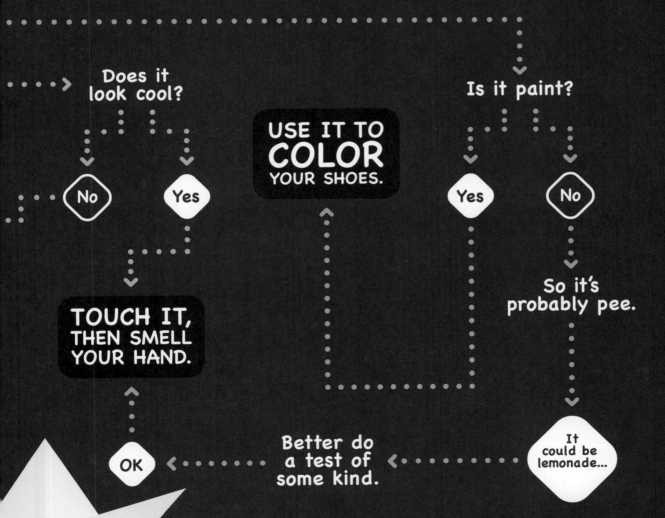

Does it
look cool?

USE IT TO
COLOR
YOUR SHOES.

Is it paint?

No   Yes

Yes   No

TOUCH IT,
THEN SMELL
YOUR HAND.

So it's
probably pee.

OK   Better do
a test of
some kind.

It
could be
lemonade...

HOW DO I GE
BACK TO SLE

Do you need Mom or Dad?

Have you tried counting sheep? → **YES**

→ **NO**

YES

NO → Give it a shot. → **OK**

Do they need to be awake, too? → **YES** → Do you want them to freak out? → **YES**

NO

NOT REALLY

Quietly stand at the side of their bed until one of them notices you.

Carefully get into their bed.

GOT IT

THERE'S NO ROOM

Throw a few elbows, they'll move.

36,041

36,042

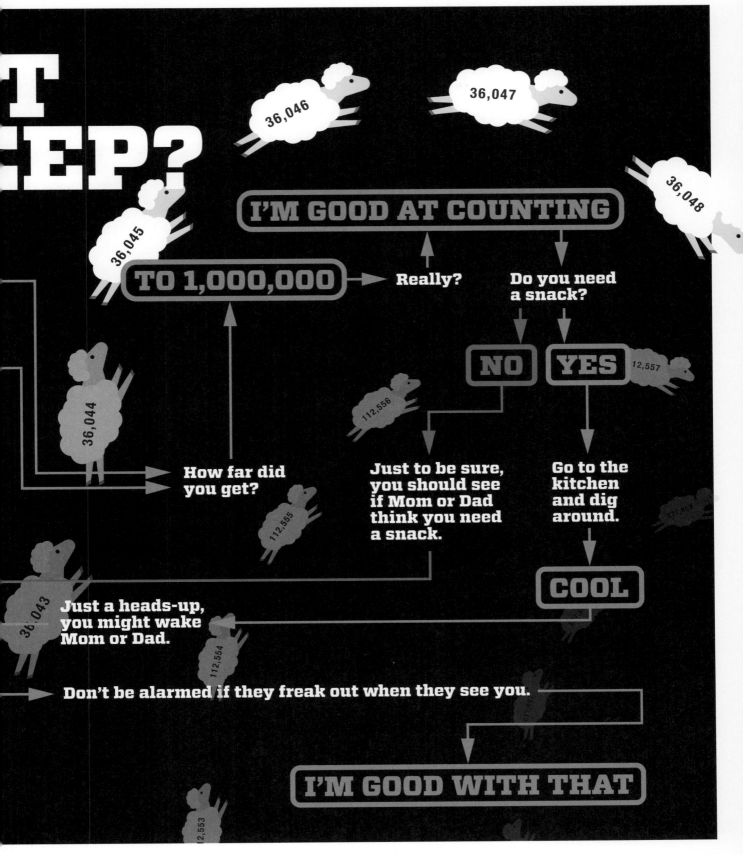

EP?

36,046

36,047

36,048

36,045

I'M GOOD AT COUNTING

TO 1,000,000 → Really? Do you need a snack?

36,044

NO YES 12,557

112,556

How far did you get?

Just to be sure, you should see if Mom or Dad think you need a snack.

Go to the kitchen and dig around.

112,555

COOL

36,043 Just a heads-up, you might wake Mom or Dad.

112,554

Don't be alarmed if they freak out when they see you.

I'M GOOD WITH THAT

12,553

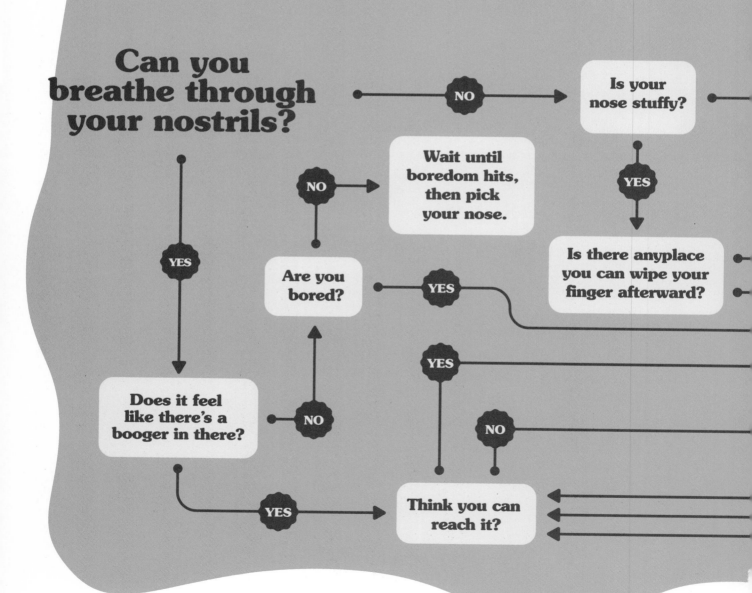

SHO
PICK M

Can you breathe through your nostrils?

NO → Is your nose stuffy?

YES

Wait until boredom hits, then pick your nose.

NO →

Is there anyplace you can wipe your finger afterward?

YES

Are you bored?

YES →

YES

Does it feel like there's a booger in there?

NO

NO

YES →

Think you can reach it?

...OULD I ...MY NOSE?

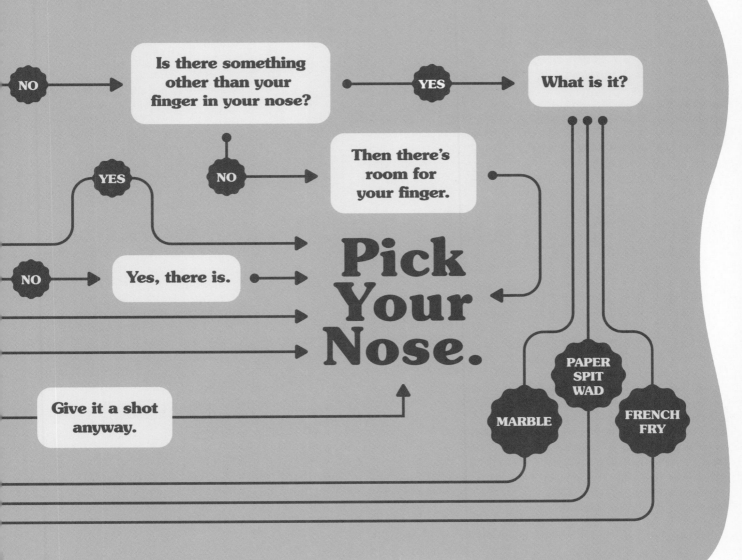

NO → Is there something other than your finger in your nose? → YES → What is it?

YES

NO → Then there's room for your finger.

NO → Yes, there is.

Pick Your Nose.

Give it a shot anyway.

PAPER SPIT WAD

MARBLE

FRENCH FRY

What Noise Should I Make from the Backseat?

Are you tired?

- NO
  - Who's driving?
    - MOM → Fart sounds
    - DAD
    - Are you hungry?
- SORT OF
- YES
  - How much longer is the trip going to take?
    - A FEW MINUTES
    - FOREVER

NO

Robot bleeps and clicks

SO HUNGRY

Fake crying

WITH MY MOUTH, ARMPIT, OR BUTT?

Sing "Pop Goes the Weasel" over and over

THAT'S NOT TECHNICALLY A NOISE, THOUGH.

Whooshing sounds every time you pass a tree or car

Sustained general whimpering

Dealer's choice

He won't make that distinction.

59

When Should I Tell Mom I Have to Pee?

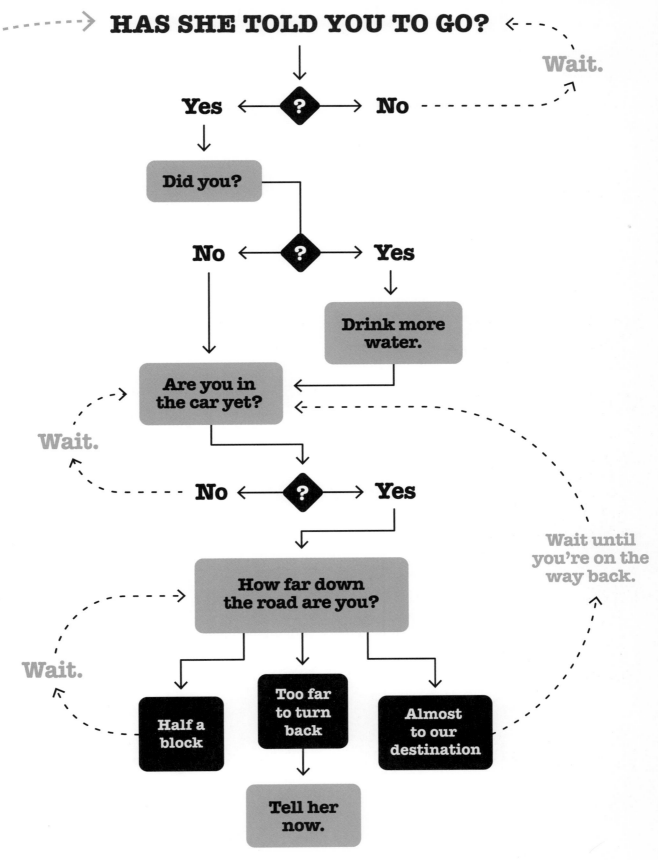

HAS SHE TOLD YOU TO GO?

? → **Yes** / **No** · · · · · → *Wait.*

Yes → **Did you?**

Did you? → **?** → **No** / **Yes**

Yes → **Drink more water.**

No → **Are you in the car yet?**

Wait.

Are you in the car yet? → **?** → **No** / **Yes**

No · · · → *Wait.*

Yes → **How far down the road are you?**

Wait until you're on the way back.

Wait.

How far down the road are you? → **Half a block** / **Too far to turn back** / **Almost to our destination**

Too far to turn back → **Tell her now.**

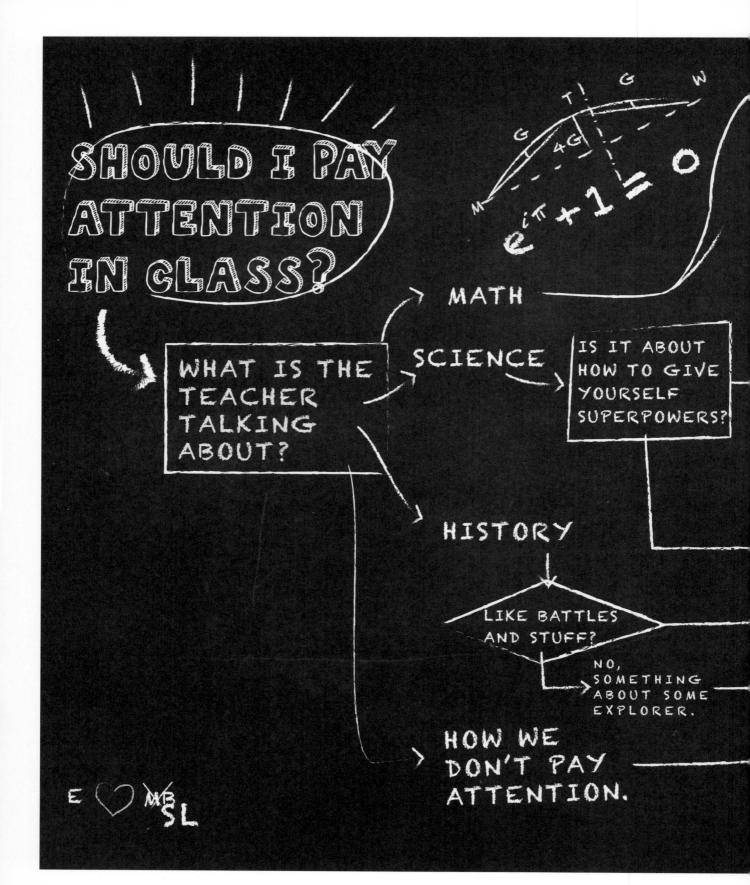

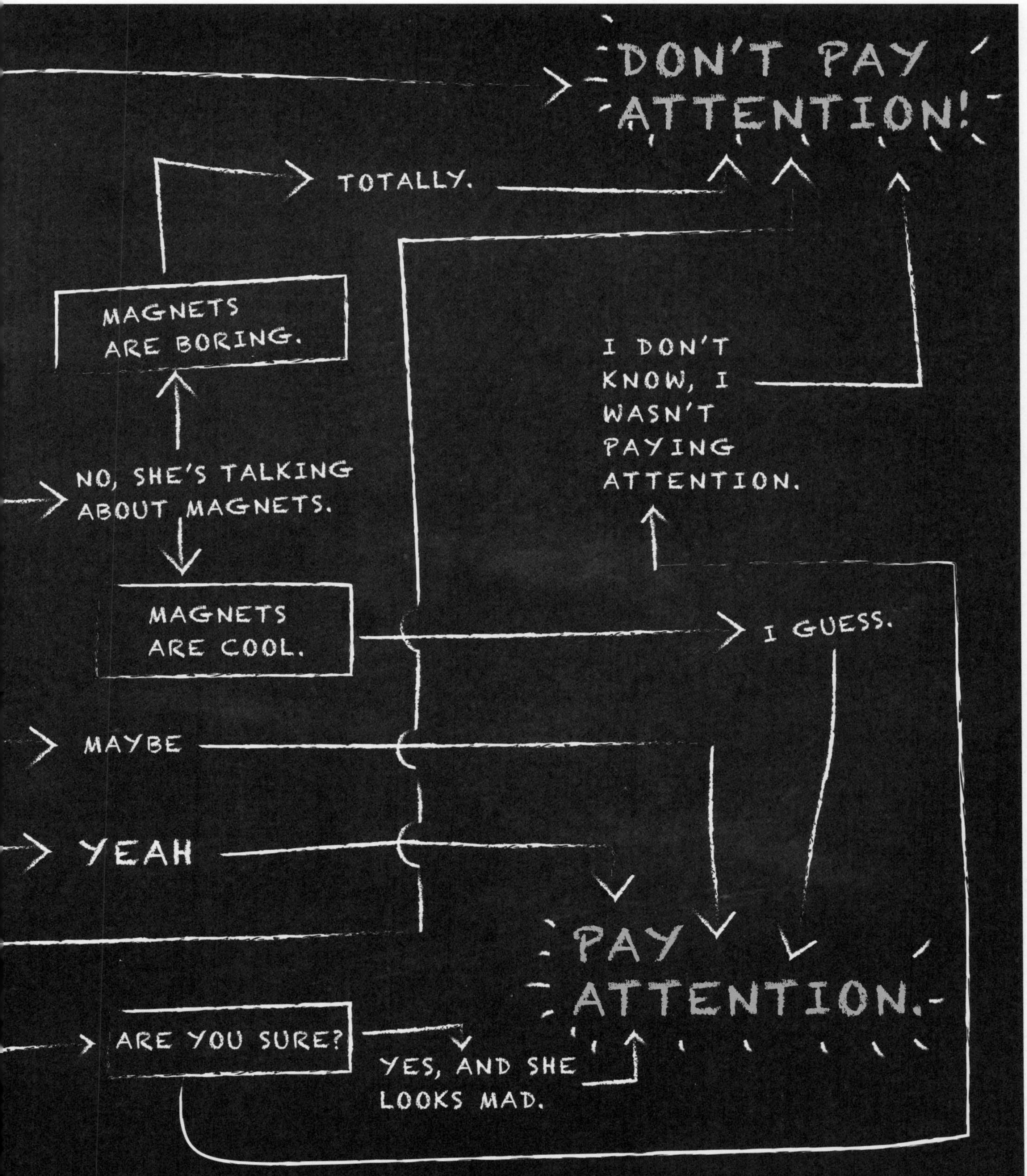
DON'T PAY ATTENTION!
TOTALLY.
MAGNETS ARE BORING.
I DON'T KNOW, I WASN'T PAYING ATTENTION.
NO, SHE'S TALKING ABOUT MAGNETS.
MAGNETS ARE COOL.
I GUESS.
MAYBE
YEAH
PAY ATTENTION.
ARE YOU SURE?
YES, AND SHE LOOKS MAD.

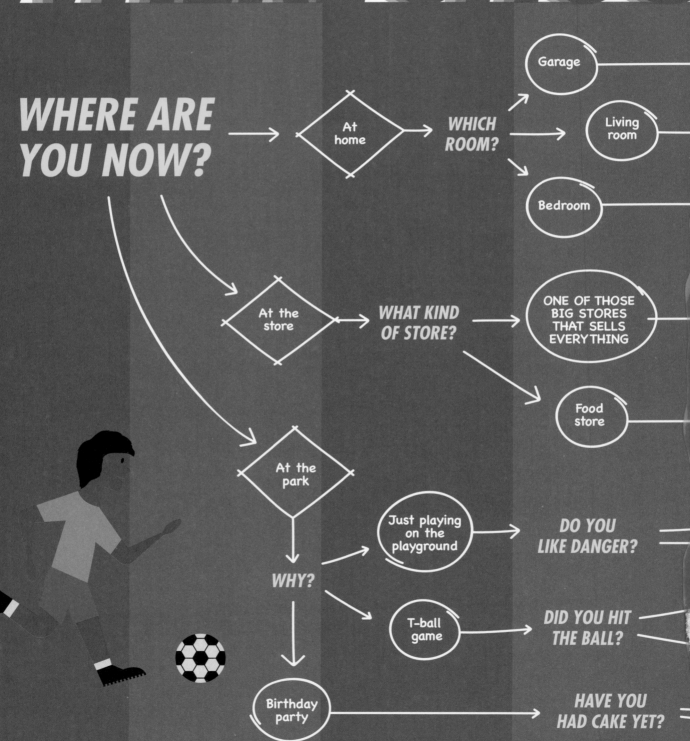

WHERE ARE YOU NOW?

At home → WHICH ROOM? → Garage / Living room / Bedroom

At the store → WHAT KIND OF STORE? → ONE OF THOSE BIG STORES THAT SELLS EVERYTHING / Food store

At the park → WHY? →
- Just playing on the playground → DO YOU LIKE DANGER?
- T-ball game → DID YOU HIT THE BALL?
- Birthday party → HAVE YOU HAD CAKE YET?

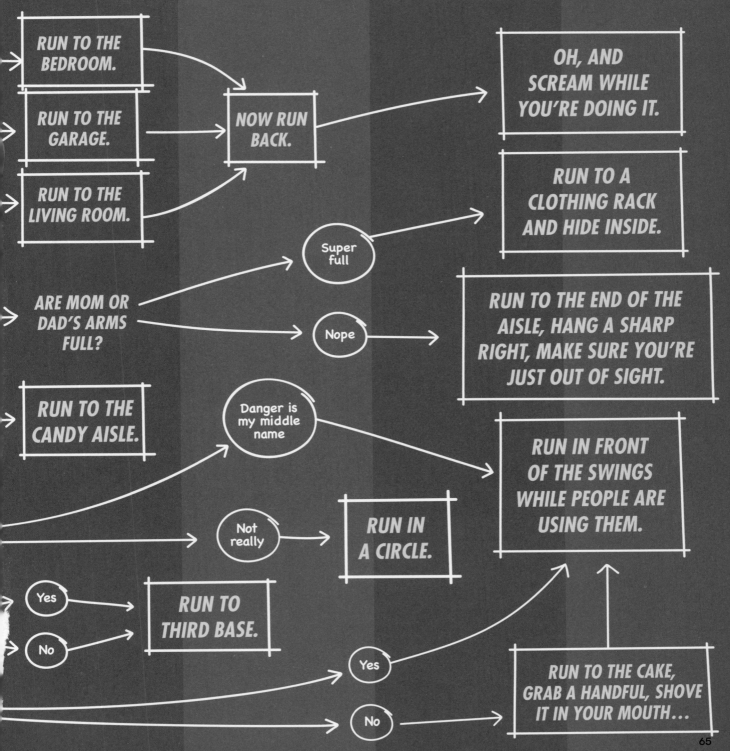

RUN TO THE BEDROOM.

RUN TO THE GARAGE.

RUN TO THE LIVING ROOM.

NOW RUN BACK.

OH, AND SCREAM WHILE YOU'RE DOING IT.

RUN TO A CLOTHING RACK AND HIDE INSIDE.

Super full

ARE MOM OR DAD'S ARMS FULL?

Nope

RUN TO THE END OF THE AISLE, HANG A SHARP RIGHT, MAKE SURE YOU'RE JUST OUT OF SIGHT.

RUN TO THE CANDY AISLE.

Danger is my middle name

RUN IN FRONT OF THE SWINGS WHILE PEOPLE ARE USING THEM.

Not really

RUN IN A CIRCLE.

Yes

No

RUN TO THIRD BASE.

Yes

No

RUN TO THE CAKE, GRAB A HANDFUL, SHOVE IT IN YOUR MOUTH...

Which Color Marker Should I Use on the Wall?

Thomas the Tank Engine or Doc McStuffins?

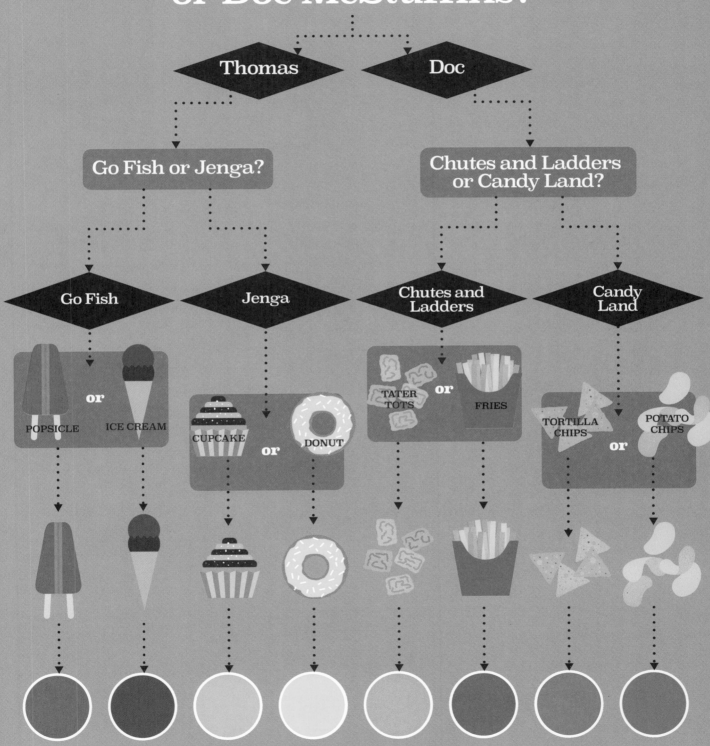

Thomas

Doc

Go Fish or Jenga?

Chutes and Ladders or Candy Land?

Go Fish

Jenga

Chutes and Ladders

Candy Land

POPSICLE

ICE CREAM

or

CUPCAKE

or

DONUT

TATER TOTS

or

FRIES

TORTILLA CHIPS

or

POTATO CHIPS

SHOULD I EAT

IS IT MAC & CHEESE?

NO.

YES!

YES!

WOULD KETCHUP MAKE IT BETTER?

IS IT GREEN?

NO.

NO.

IS IT A COOKIE?

THIS FOOD?

NO.

YES!

PUT KETCHUP ON IT...

THEN...

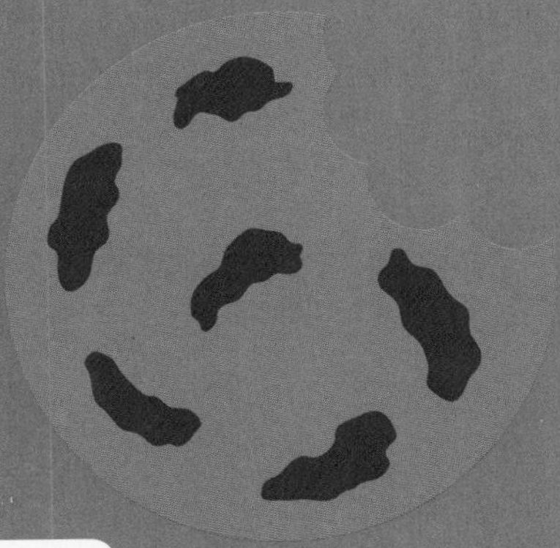

YES!

EAT IT.

DON'T EAT IT.

WHAT WOULD I DO WITH A GIANT ROBOT?

DO YOU LIKE HELPING PEOPLE?

YES

NO

CAN THE ROBOT FLY?

YES

NO

DOES IT CHANGE INTO SOMETHING COOL, LIKE A HELICOPTER OR TANK?

NO

YEAH, A HELICOPTER.

FLY AROUND THE CITY LOOKING FOR CITIZENS IN DANGER TO RESCUE.

STOMP ON CARS.

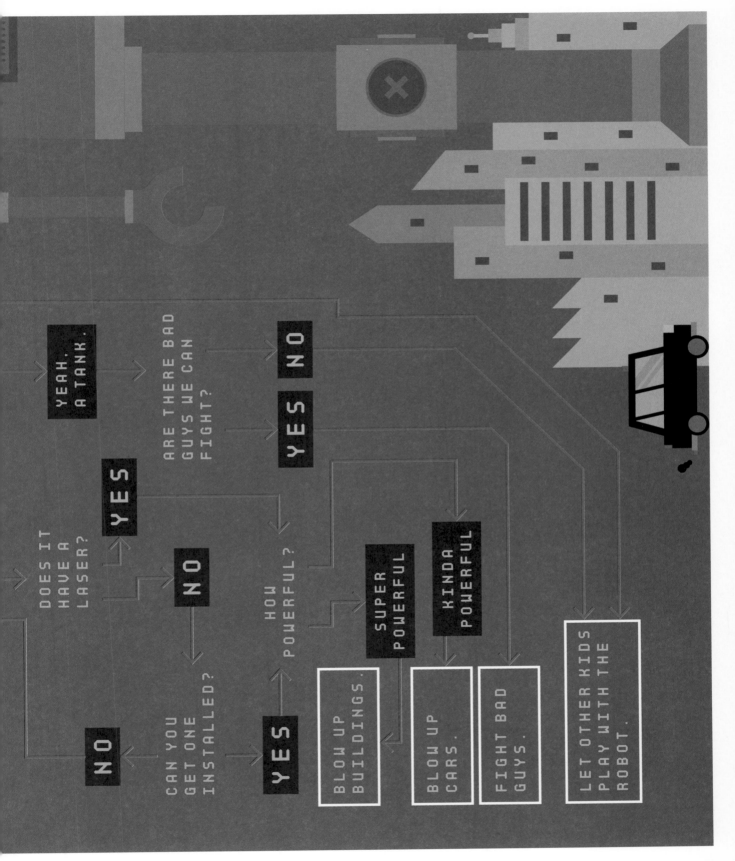

DOES IT HAVE A LASER?

YEAH, A TANK.

YES

NO

CAN YOU GET ONE INSTALLED?

YES

NO

ARE THERE BAD GUYS WE CAN FIGHT?

YES NO

HOW POWERFUL?

SUPER POWERFUL

KINDA POWERFUL

BLOW UP BUILDINGS.

BLOW UP CARS.

FIGHT BAD GUYS.

LET OTHER KIDS PLAY WITH THE ROBOT.

SHOULD I WATCH

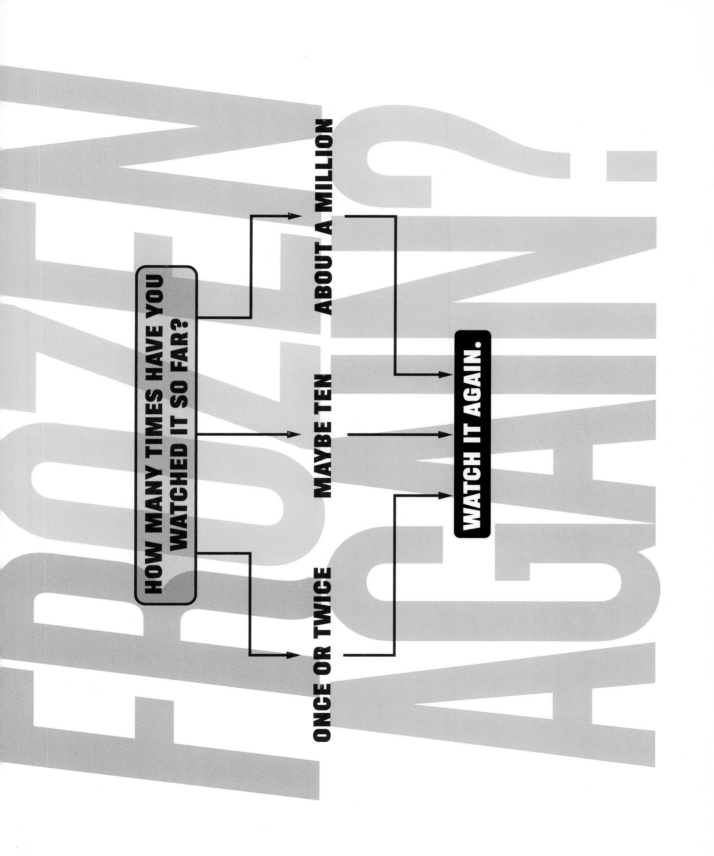

FROZEN AGAIN?

HOW MANY TIMES HAVE YOU WATCHED IT SO FAR?

ABOUT A MILLION

MAYBE TEN

ONCE OR TWICE

WATCH IT AGAIN.

Do I love my parents?

Do they yell?

ALL THE TIME

SOME-TIMES

About what?

What else do they do?

ME SPILLING GRAPE JUICE ON THE COUCH AGAIN

HOW I DON'T GET MY SHOES ON FAST ENOUGH.

ME PLAYING KICKBALL IN THE HOUSE

ARE WE THERE YET?